Making Grapevine Wreaths

Gayle O'Donnell

Contents

❧ Making Grapevine Wreaths ❧

For nearly twenty years, I've dabbled in everything from sewing, crocheting, and needlework to pottery, macramé and leathercrafts. In later years, I took up basketry and broom making. But never before have I found something as enjoyable and interesting as crafting with grapevine. Grapevine grows wild and is naturally abundant. Grapevines are easy to find and pick, and easy and fun to work with, as you'll discover.

After reading this booklet, you will be able to take a pile of freshly cut grapevine branches and design beautiful wreaths of many sizes, shapes, and patterns. My instructions are simple and basic. Anyone can create with grapevine and make unique, original, and natural gifts and decorations with hardly any tools or money.

I now invite you to explore the fascinating and natural world of grapevine and enjoy discovering what you can design and create from nature.

🌺 All About Grapevine 🌺

The grape is a wild, thornless, woody, high-climbing, long-living vine of many varieties found in the woods and thickets, bottomlands, and streambanks, fertile and sandy soils throughout the country. It can be found tumbling over fences and stone walls, weaving itself through bushes, and hanging like ropes from tall trees. Grapevine climbs by means of tendrils. A tendril is actually a leafless stem, which twirls and coils itself around a support like a tree branch or another part of the grapevine. The first explorers of North America found so much wild grapevine that they named the new land Vineland. Grapes are cultivated throughout the world for use by the wine industry. The famous Concord grape and other cultivated varieties were developed from the wild fox grape or North American grape.

The wild grapevine generally appears as a stringy, woody, tangled web of reddish-brown twigs and branches, which seem to grow every which way. The vines are always visible throughout the seasons. Young leaves sprouting off the bare vines appear pinkish towards the middle to the end of April depending on where you live, becoming large and round, toothed, sometimes heart-shaped and often lobed as they mature. They form heavy, leafy canopies by summertime as they drape themselves over bushes and stone walls and hang from trees. In the autumn the leaves turn a rich yellow color, then drop to reveal their delicious fruits, exposing the abundant reddish-brown vines among the vegetation.

The grapes are bluish-black, ripening generally in September, sometimes by the end of August. When ripe, their aroma fills the air! Many songbirds and animals feed on the wild grapes, such as grouse, partridge, pheasant, wild turkey, skunk, fox, raccoon, rabbit, squirrel, possum, and coyote.

There is quite a wide variety of wild grapes: chicken, fox, possum, cat, river, summer, winter, frost, bull, pigeon, bunch, muscadine, scuppernong, New England, silverleaf, postoak, dune, sand, and bush. Wild grapes make delicious wine, juice, jelly, and preserves. Grapes are rich in iron and vitamins and are a source of instant energy. They are delicious eaten plain right off the vine, or can be sun-dried for future use. The leaves can be stuffed or rolled. Ancient herbal practitioners prescribed the dried fruit for chest disorders, the leaves were used for wounds, and branch ashes for whitening teeth.

Grapevine comes in all shapes, sizes, and lengths; in shades of reddish-browns, tans, greens, and greys. There is a very old vine that is as thick as a baseball bat, vine so long that kids can swing on it, and vine as thin as yarn. It can have all kinds of natural bends, twists, and angles. Older vine can be rather long, thick, and branched. It usually has a couple of layers of bark, the outer bark being loose and shaggy. The vine underneath is generally of a tan color. Despite their size, the older vines are amazingly flexible.

Young vines are the newer shoots which haven't had many years in the elements. There is usually a single, tough, stringy layer of bark in shades of browns to reds to purples, and some varieties have a waxy feel to the bark. These vines are generally less branched, can be quite long, and have wonderful new curling tendrils. Underneath the bark, the vine is very green. This vine is still flexible but it does tend to break more easily. Vines can take on a silver-grey color from being very old and weathered, the same way cedar and other woods change color with age.

Picking Attire

Picking attire for collecting grapevine should consist of old clothes including long pants, long sleeves, and gloves to avoid cuts, scratches, splinters, and the like. Don't wear a sweater because the vine's branches and tendrils will get hooked in it and everything else, from clothes to jewelry to glasses to shoelaces. It is not a bad idea to wear eye protection to guard from falling debris or being poked in the eye with a branch.

The vines should be gathered fresh. Some sources suggest soaking vines that are not fresh in water until pliable, but I find it just as easy to pick fresh vines. The vines are flexible, pliable, and can be bent and twisted quite easily. As they dry out, they keep their shape very well. The vines don't have to be used immediately. After it is picked, the vine can remain outside unused for a few weeks, more or less, depending on the size of the vine and the weather. The thicker and heavier the vine is, the longer it can sit outside, especially if the weather is cold and/or wet. The thinner the vine and the drier and hotter the weather is, the more quickly it will dry out. As long as there is some flexibility to a cut vine there is no problem in using it. You'll know soon enough if it is too dry as you use it.

The ideal and the most pleasant time for gathering vines is in the fall. By this time the big yellow leaves have nearly all dropped or they come off easily when the vine is pulled down, and the juicy purple grapes are ripe for picking, if the birds and animals haven't gotten to them first. I continue to pick grapevine throughout the winter, though not nearly as much as in the fall.

The leaves begin to bud about mid-April, and the vines are still easy to find and gather. But, as spring turns to summer, the leaves quickly grow rather large, new shoots sprout, and suddenly there is lush, green growth everywhere. The big leaves, long shoots, and new tendrils make the vines very heavy, and if picked during the summer, you must cut off and discard this new growth — none of it is good for crafting. New green shoots are too fleshy, like plant stems, and they have yet to develop the layer of bark which begins to appear later in the fall. The leaves can be used for rolling or stuffing, however.

Locating Grapevine

Locating patches of grapevine is easy. Friends, relatives, or neighbors may have grapevines on their property. Take a walk in the woods; take a ride down an old country road. Scan the roadsides. Look up at the trees and into the bushes. In the summer, the size and appearance of the leaves stand out among the surrounding vegetation. Look for the heavy, leafy canopies formed by all the new growth. In late fall and winter look for the stringy, reddish-brown, web-like growth. Think of it as the plant's skeleton. The color stands out well against stone walls, bare shrubbery, and the greyish trees, and even more so against the white snow.

After finding a good patch of grapevine in the autumn,

the first thing you should do is to get permission to pick, if possible. Most of the time, if you ask a landowner if you may trim his vines, he won't object. Then, stand back and study the area for a moment. You must be sure you are picking fresh live vine and not old dead vine. From a distance, you can't really tell after the leaves are gone unless you remember seeing leaves during the summer. You'll have no trouble spotting live areas of grapevine during the growing season, but after the leaves and grapes have dropped, the only way to tell is to feel and bend the vine. Live, fresh vine bends without breaking, and when cut, looks green and moist inside. Old dead vine is brown, dry, and brittle, and is not useful for crafting.

Scatter your picking areas so that the vine has time to grow back, which it seems to do rather quickly. I have found that I can go back to many areas year after year, picking the new growth and older growth that I had missed or bypassed a year or two before. You also may find different varieties of grapevine by picking in other areas. Other varieties may have different colored vines or bark, different textures or appearances, different shaped leaves, and different lengths of vine.

Cutting Grapevine

Focus on just one branch and trace it to its beginning. It may be growing directly from the ground or it may keep branching off larger and thicker sections of vine. It may grow one hundred feet straight up into a tree or it may be short and full of branches that cover fences, stone walls, and bushes, depending on what it has to climb on.

With a pair of clippers, cut the vine at the thickness you want. Don't pull it up out of the ground — as long as you don't uproot the vine, it will grow back. Then start to yank, jerk, pull, and tug until the vine loosens and can be pulled free. Each time one vine is freed, you'll discover many more vines that were buried or hidden. Beware of pulling grapevine from dead tree limbs. A good strong vine will bring the dead wood along with it, and sometimes an entire dead tree!

If the grapevine you want is climbing high up in a tree, first try to pull it down instead of cutting it. That way, if you can't pull it down, at least it can continue to grow and produce grapes. If you cut it and then can't free it, it is a waste. If you are pulling on a vine that has a few branches, try loosening one branch at a time.

Grapevines, and any other vines that climb by tendrils, are generally very easy to pull down because the tendrils are the part of the vine which attach and curl around other branches and such. Vines without tendrils such as bittersweet, twist and twine their stems around themselves and other branches, and cannot be pulled down easily.

🌸 Preparing Your Vines 🌸

Grapevine may look like a tangled, stringy mess, but it really isn't, and all of its different parts have great crafting potential. Some vines may have a lot of branches, some may be long and single, while others may be very heavy or very thin. I have found uses and projects for all of these vines.

After picking and transporting the vines to a working area, the process of cleaning, separating, and sorting begins. There sits a mountain of grapevines just waiting to be lovingly crafted and woven into all kinds of beautiful wreaths, baskets, and unique works of art, but first it must be divided up into some kind of manageable amounts. It is much easier to work if you can see what you have to work with.

I start by pulling out and cleaning the thickest, heaviest vines and putting them in one pile. Cleaning is nothing more than cutting off any smaller unwanted branches, broken, or dead ends, leaves, and so on. The longest and biggest of the heavy vines, about one-half inch up to about three-quarters of an inch in diameter, are mostly used for weaving giant outdoor wreaths for houses, garages, or barns. These huge vines, which tend to be long, old, shaggy, and without many tendrils, are amazingly flexible despite their size, and it's fun to see what monster creations you can make!

Next, I take all of the leftover branches of vine, examine and clean each one individually, and then see what each branch has to offer. If there are any long, thin, single vines sprouting off a branch, I clip them off and make a second pile. These single vines, similar in thickness to heavy twine, are ideal for basket weft, delicate heart wreaths, tiny wreaths, lashing or sewing, or other small projects.

The vine branches that are left over go into a third pile of medium-sized (about the thickness of a pen or pencil), approximately five feet in length or longer, branched or single. These pieces can be used for almost any wreathmaking. Branched vines make nice, full wreaths. Other vine branches may be good for solid wreaths or smaller wreaths.

As you can see, very little goes to waste!

Supplies and Equipment

Now that the vines have been sorted, it is time to design and create. There is no need to go out and buy any special tools for crafting with grapevine. You probably have most of these things around your house or workshop.

Garden Clippers. These are perfect for grapevines, from cutting down the vines to clipping off dead or broken branches to trimming your creation. A good, heavy pair of scissors will work just as well.

Pliers. Regular pliers are useful when making forms out of coat hangers. Needlenose pliers may come in handy to insert or pull out a vine you can't grasp with your fingers.

Masking Tape. Masking tape can temporarily hold grapevine pieces together until they are secured by wrapping or weaving. Cut off or pick out once the area is held together.

Awl or Screwdriver. The awl or any long thin instrument can be used to open up a passageway between vines for inserting another vine.

Coathangers. These can be bent into a variety of shapes with a pair of pliers and wrapped in thin vine.

Hot Glue Gun. A good tool for attaching decorations to grapevine, but use with care — hot glue can burn. Use a stick to push the glued pieces together instead of your finger.

Tacky Glue. A good, clear-drying glue for attaching decorations to grapevine, but slow-drying.

Unscented Hairspray. An inexpensive way to apply a layer of lacquer to dried flowers, weeds, and such with fuzzy or flyaway flowers or seed pods.

TIPS FOR WORKING WITH GRAPEVINES

- Grapevine creations are meant to be uneven, irregular, imperfect, even lopsided. Its natural state and beauty should be stressed.

- Pick fresh, live vine. It is quite flexible and can be bent, shaped, and twisted easily. Dead grapevine is of no use.

- Begin with the thicker end or butt end of the vine and work towards the thinner end or the tip.

- Incorporate natural bends, angles, and forks into your project for shaping and added reinforcement.

- Spend time searching through the piles of vine for a particular piece that will work well for what you are doing — a certain thickness, a certain length, a fork, and so on.

- To remove bark from the vine easily, gently bend the vine back and forth so the bark cracks and separates.

- Young vine is sometimes very long and thin, great for small wreaths and rings, but it snaps more easily than older vine.

- Try to readjust your wrapping to avoid placing the knobs on a curve or a bend. Breakage will occur if you try to make the vine bend on or near the knobby areas from where the tendrils or stems sprout. It will bend nicely between the knobs.

- You can pull and twist the vine just so far before it cracks, splits, or breaks. By working with the vine, and with time, patience, and practice, you will develop a feel for the material and discover just how far it will go, what it can do, and how to maneuver it.

- If your vine does break at any point, simply tuck the broken end into the weaving, and begin in that general area with another piece of vine.

- In wreathmaking, start a bit smaller than the size you wish to end up with. Wreaths tend to increase in size as you wrap and add vines.

- Often, some of the tendrils will get buried as you wrap and twist the vines. Pick and stretch them out as you go along if you want them exposed. When making a wreath, determine which side is the front and bend the tendrils on the backside toward the center or to the sides. Cut off any tendrils that will prevent the wreath from laying flat against a wall.

❧ Designing Wreaths ❧

Traditionally, wreaths have been a part of the holiday season, but the use of wreaths goes back to ancient cultures. The Greeks and Romans used them as head-dresses or head garlands made out of leaves, greens, and tree boughs such as olive, laurel, oak, pine, holly, and mistletoe. The ancient Olympians were given wreaths of olive or laurel as their prizes, Jesus wore a wreath or crown of thorns, and both Julius Caesar and Napoleon wore crowns of laurel, which symbolized triumph and eternity.

Crown comes from the Latin word, *corona*, which means wreath, crown, or garland, and the circle symbolizes eternity. Wreaths have been worn by royalty for centuries, and by the addition of jewels, stones, and metals, have become the ornate crowns we associate with royalty today. Unfortunately, it is not clear as to when wreaths as head ornaments became home and wall decorations.

Wreaths are no longer limited to front door decorations. Today wreaths of all shapes, color combinations, and sizes can be found in every room of the house; as well as in churches, offices, banks, restaurants, and other businesses. They appear in all decorating styles and in every season of the year.

A grapevine wreath has a pleasing natural look that is so popular these days. And because it is natural, there is no need to strive for perfection. No wreath or grapevine creation can or should be perfectly even, perfectly round. But it will be perfectly natural and unique. There is no right or wrong way to craft with vines, so it is impossible to make a "bad" wreath!

A grapevine wreath, whether simply decorated with a full paper bow, serving as a frame for pictures, mirrors, little scenes or still lifes, or gracing a table as a unique centerpiece, can go as far as your imagination and creativity allow. The possibilities are endless! Now get the clippers ready.

Round and Full Wreath

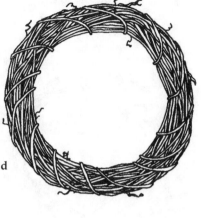

Materials needed

    clippers
    some medium-weight branched
      vines approximately 6 feet
      or more in length
    a few long, single vines

1. Select two or three vines, line up the butt ends together, and hold them all in one bundle. Bring the ends
   around to form a circle and make a simple overhand
   knot. The circle will stay together and you can check
   your measurement. Pull the knot tighter if you want a
   smaller wreath, let it out a little if it is not big enough.

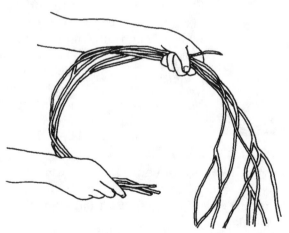

*Start with two or three vines, butt ends together. Form a circle
and make a simple overhand knot.*

2. Coil the remaining vines around the circle you just made, grasping the vine circle in one hand as you coil with the other. (Think of the way you would coil up a length of hose or rope.) Tuck the ends of the vines into the circle. Your wreath may or may not be as thick as you want it, depending on the lengths of the vines you started with. For more fullness, add another few vines. Insert the thicker ends into the circle and coil these vines around in the same manner as before, tucking in the ends. Now you have a loose circle of vines which has to be held together somehow.

3. Next, select a long single length of vine. This piece will be used to wrap in and out around the circle, holding the vines and any loose ends all together. Tuck the thicker end of this vine into the circle, finding a snug spot. Grasp the other end and begin to thread it in and out, in and out, all around the circle of vines. Go around as many times as you can with that piece. When it runs out, tuck the end into the wreath, again finding a snug spot.

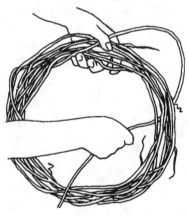

No one can tell you when your wreath is done. It's all up to you. A wreath is finished when you like it, when its appearance is pleasing to you. Then give it a final trim, as much or as little as you like.

A second method to achieve a full wreath is by piling up single rings or circles of vine. This is a method I use when the vines are not long enough to coil or when I accumulate a lot of short, leftover pieces. As long as the vine is long enough to make a knot, you can make a single ring; and a pile of rings will make a wreath.

For a 12-inch diameter wreath, make a variety of circles between 10 and 12 inches across. Pile them all up together until it appears to be the thickness you want, staggering the knot areas. Then continue as in step 3 by selecting a long single vine to wrap in and out around all the rings.

Simply insert the end into the pile of rings you are holding and thread this piece in and out, going completely around a few times until all rings and ends are secured.

Variations

- Vary the tension of the wrapping vine in step 3. By wrapping it loosely, your wreath will look lighter and fuller. By pulling it tighter, the wreath will be more compact.
- Vary the thickness or appearance of the wrapping vine. A much thicker wrapping vine around a circle of many thin vines will emphasize the pattern of the wrap. A stripped green vine, a shaggy brown vine or a silver-grey vine can also be wrapped around the vine circle to emphasize different colors and textures.
- Vary the direction and placement of the wrapping vine. By adding additional vines and wrapping in opposite directions, you can create a variety of patterns. Also, the number of times the vine is wrapped around the circle adds to the pattern. Let your creativity go wild — experiment with thicknesses and colors of vine in different combinations for a variety of patterns and appearances.

Using a larger wrapping vine

Round and Solid Wreath

Materials needed

clippers
long, single vines of medium weight or more

1. Beginning with one length of vine, form a circle and make a simple overhand knot. Check your measurement.

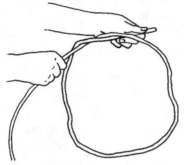

2. Grasp the far end of the vine and immediately begin to thread it in and out, in and out, twisting the vine around itself. Tuck the end into the twisting vines as you come to the end of that length. If you clip the end at an angle it will slide between the vines more easily.

3. Add another single length of vine by cutting that end at an angle and sliding the pointed end into any snug spot created by the twisting vines in the area you ended. This is where those knobby areas of the vine are helpful — they can help to wedge the new piece

in. Keep pushing the vine into a space until the knobs get caught inside and it is hard to pull the vine out.

4. Continue threading this vine in and out following in the same direction, and tuck the end in as before. Repeat this step until your wreath is as big as you want it to be. The more pieces you add, the heavier, sturdier, and wider it becomes. Wreaths made this way look tight and solid, with a spiraling and rope-like pattern. It is possible to make a wreath from one exceptionally long piece of vine!

Variations

- For a two-layer look, wrap a wreath all in one direction as above. Then take an additional length of vine or two and wrap in the opposite direction for the second layer. You can wrap as few or as many times around as you like. Again this is where you can let your creativity run wild. You can always unwrap the vine and try something else if you don't like the pattern you have created.

- For an open but still solid appearance, keep alternating directions each time a new vine is added. The multi-layered result gives an interesting, criss-crossing pattern.

- Experiment with peeled vines. Removing all the bark and cutting off any tendrils will give you a very smooth, wooden, clean-looking wreath and will emphasize the pattern better than shaggy vines.

Criss-cross Wrapped Wreath

Oval Wreath

This is a very easy wreath shape to achieve, and it offers more ways to decorate because it can be hung horizontally or vertically. As with any other wreath, design it the way you want to — large or small, tight or loose, shaggy or peeled.

One way to form an oval is simply to push it into shape while you are making the wreath. Because the vines are still fresh and green, they can be pushed, pulled, and somewhat molded into shapes. Begin with a round wreath and after you've made a few rounds, simply grasp the sides of your wreath with your hands and push toward the middle until your desired oval shape is created. Continue to wrap and push, wrap and push, until your wreath is completed. As it dries, the shape will remain.

Another way to shape an oval is to incorporate a naturally

Tie a rope around the middle of a newly-made round wreath to create an oval.

curved piece of grapevine into the wreath. You may have come across one while sorting the vines. This piece can be added to strengthen the curve of the oval.

You can make an oval wreath out of a newly finished round wreath by tying it into shape. Wrap a piece of rope or strong twine around the middle, and tie it up as the wreath becomes the oval shape you desire. Let it dry a few days before removing the rope.

Teardrop Wreath

A teardrop-shaped wreath is an-other unique design; decorate it point up or point down. This is a perfect example of what a vine with a wide fork or natural angle can be used for. While sorting the grapevines, you should have come across quite a few vines with natural right angles or wide forks.

1. Select a good-size medium weight vine which has either a sharp angle or wide fork. Trim off any unwanted branches.

2. This wreath is also started by the knot method, just as the previous wreaths were, but the beginning vine has the angle. As you wrap and add additional vines, the natural angle will keep the point sharp. An additional angled piece or two may be added to reinforce the point. Once again, you may use single vines, heavy vines, or branched vines, you can wrap it tight or loose, you may criss-cross or follow one direction, just as long as you include natural right angles to make the point sharp.

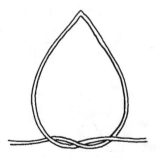

🌸 Hearts 🌸

Heart wreaths are not hard to do and can be fashioned in a variety of ways, from dainty to giant, depending on what kind of vine you use.

The first heart wreath illustrated here is made from very thin, long vines wrapped over a wire form — enough to cover the wire but not so much that it loses its delicate appearance. This is the only wreath done on a wire form because the thin vines are not strong enough to make their own form, as the other wreaths do. A regular all-metal coat hanger makes a perfect twelve-inch heart form. Coat hangers can be bent into other shapes and wrapped in vines if you care to experiment with them. As with any other wreath, design it your own way. Even though thin vine is used here, it still can be peeled or shaggy, with or without tendrils, wrapped in one direction or both, all giving different looks and patterns.

The rest of the hearts are designed from the other sizes of vines. A quick, rustic heart with a tail can be made with short leftovers and branched pieces. Much larger hearts can be constructed from the heavy vines.

You may at some point want to try making a monstrous three-, four-, or even five-foot heart wreath, perfect for outside on a barn, garage, or your home. By following the directions for the giant heart, you can. The only difference is the size of the vine. The larger the project is, the larger the vine should be, just as smaller projects need smaller vine. The thick vines are long, awkward and heavy in weight. It is not a hard wreath to construct, but it requires some physical strength to maneuver the enormous vines around. Jump in and give it a try — you may surprise yourself with what you can do; you may even come up with a heart design of your own!

Thin and Dainty Heart

Materials needed

    coat hanger
    pliers
    clippers
    a pile of long, thin, single
        vines approximately 6 to
        8 feet in length or longer

1. Make a heart form out of a coat hanger: Hook your
   index finger on the bottom of the hanger (a) midway
   from the ends and pull down (fig. 1). This makes the
   bottom point of the heart. With pliers, round out sides
   (b and c) to form the curves of the heart (fig. 2).

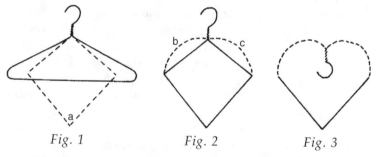

Fig. 1   Fig. 2   Fig. 3

    Flip the top of the hanger to the inside (fig. 3) and
   finish rounding out the curves evenly. Bend the hook
   back and forth until it breaks off.

2. Starting at the bottom point of the
   heart form, simply twist the vine in
   and out around the frame, leaving
   the end sticking out about an inch,
   until you come around to the
   center point.

3. Using your hand to guide the vine, make a loop around  the point. (A loop is nothing more than the bottom half of a "figure 8.") Remember that vines will bend best between the knobby areas. If the vine is not positioned right at this point of the construction to make a loop, slide the vine up or down a bit at the bottom to reposition it.

4. Continue wrapping in and out around the other side of the form until you end up back at the bottom point where you started. Round one complete.

5. Give the vine the slightest bend with your fingers so it is positioned upward and continue wrapping tightly around the wire for the second time around. When the vine ends, tuck it between the twisting vines, insert another length and continue. Try to make good loops around the top point. If possible, reposition or rewrap the vine so you can get a nice bend. If you can't, don't worry about it. If the vine should break while forming a loop, just tuck the end in and start fresh with another piece of vine. The subsequent loops should be placed higher or lower than the first one, but again you may need to reposition or rewrap the vine to avoid a bulky center area.

6. As the vines build up around the form, determine which will be the front side so you can concentrate on making sure that that side is the best one. It is easy to insert additional vines by sliding them into the loop area, or insert them into the bottom point area. Continue until the wire form is completely covered, then give it a final trimming. Should you discover a spot where the wire is still showing, simply tuck in a small stick or some bark to cover the spot.

Heart with a Tail

Materials needed

    clippers
    thin to medium-weight vines
       (leftover branches of six feet
       in length or less, single and
       branched pieces are suitable)
    a few long, single vines

1. Gather up about 10–12 pieces of
   vine, with all the tip ends together,
   into a bundle and hold it firmly
   in one hand. These ends will
   form the heart's tail.

2. Divide the bundle in half with the other hand, bending and bringing each half around evenly to form the curves of the heart. Join and hold at the bottom so that the tails are hanging downward. The tails can be as long or as short as you like, depending on the lengths of vine you start with.

3. While holding everything together firmly in one hand, take one of the long, single vines, bend it into a U shape, and wrap it around the top of your fist. Then use all your fingers to grasp and gently squeeze this vine around to the back, while squeezing the rest of the joining ends together.

4. Next, criss-cross the ends over everything in back of the heart and continue wrapping and criss-crossing up the center of the heart until it divides. Then, using each branch independently, wrap each one around the curves and down to the bottom. If your lashing vine should break, tuck the end in and start with a fresh piece. Continue adding and criss-crossing the thin vines all around the heart until it feels secure.

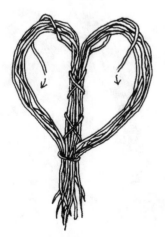

Giant Heart

Materials needed

clippers
masking tape
long, thick, single vines, some with natural angles

1. Instead of making a wire form as in the thin heart construction, we'll make the large heart form right from the heavy vine itself. Select one vine with a good right angle. Lay it on the ground or floor, and kneel or step on this piece as you begin to form the heart so both hands are free to maneuver the rest of the big vines.

2. Bend the vine (it doesn't matter which side you begin with) around to form the curve of the heart and, if the vine will cooperate and if it is positioned right, form a loop (bottom half of a "figure 8") for the center point, just as the loop was done for the thin and dainty heart. Place your palm and fingers right around the curve of the loop to help mold it, ease it, guide it, and push it around, remembering that the vine will bend very nicely between knobby areas.

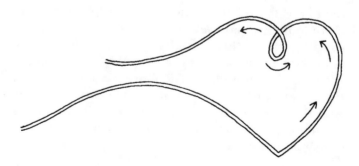

Select a vine with a good right angle, form the ends into a heart shape, making a loop at the point.

3. Form the other heart curve and head down towards the bottom point, twisting the vine around itself as it meets the other end. Your heart form is done.

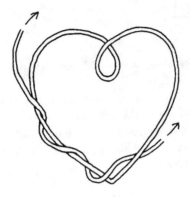

Thread one end of the vine around itself, in and out of the heart.

4. Gently bend the vine around the bottom angle with your fingers and continue upward, threading the vine in and out around itself until that piece ends. Tuck the end between the twisting vines. Then work with the other end.
5. Add another vine by cutting the end at an angle and sliding it between the twisting vines in the area you left off. Continue twisting it in the same direction or the opposite direction. You will need to make a few more loops around the center point, some higher, some lower. Do this carefully and slowly by using your whole hand and fingers to hold, squeeze and ease the vine into place. The more vines you add and twist, the sturdier and heavier your heart will become. And the more times you change direction, the wider it will become. Continue until the heart is sturdy and strong and you are happy with its appearance.

If the heart is out of shape at any point, don't be afraid to push it, pull it, bend it, or step on it to reshape it. The vine is fresh so this can easily be done. When your heart wreath is finished, reshaping can easily be done if it is necessary, as long as the form you originally started out with was equally symmetrical. Here are a few things to try:

If it doesn't lay flat, put something large like a board, heavy boxes, even rocks or cinder blocks on top of it. Check it after a few days.

Threading a broomstick horizontally through the top portion is a great help in straightening out a heart whose center tends to flip up a bit.

Wedge a stick horizontally between the center point and the side of the heart if the curves are not even. Check it after a few days.

If the angled vine is not long enough to loop right from the start but has a perfect angle to use, make only a heart form from this particular piece. Lay the angled vine on the floor or ground, step on the angle or put some kind of weight upon it. Bring both ends around to the middle, making sure the heart curves are even. Wrap up the center with masking tape. The center may flip up but that will get straightened out as you begin to wrap, twist, and loop.

Continue by using the heavy single vines, threading them in and out, around the vine form, just as the thin vines were wrapped around the wire form for the dainty heart. Use a few additional angles at the bottom point, and make the loops around the center point as with the other hearts. The masking tape can be cut or pulled out when the wreath is done.

Split Heart

Materials needed

clippers
thin to medium-weight long, single vines
one forked piece of medium-weight vine which splits evenly

1. Start with the forked piece of vine — it will make the
   form for this heart wreath, allowing you to have a
   center backbone for decorating. Trim off any unwanted
   branches. With one hand holding the main stem, bend
   each separate branch around equally, and hold all three
   ends together so it looks like a giant lollipop. You may
   temporarily bind these ends together with a piece of
   masking tape, or just keep your fist tightly closed
   around them.

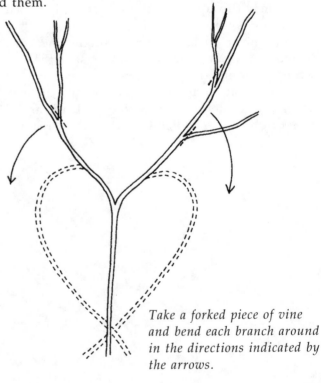

*Take a forked piece of vine
and bend each branch around
in the directions indicated by
the arrows.*

2. Twist the long, single vines around the split heart form, similar to the way the other hearts were done. Give the vine a gentle bend around the bottom point and head upward again, temporarily ignoring the original ends still sticking out. In addition to twisting the vine around the center point to make loops, you may choose to twist the vine up and down the back-bone, or disregard it completely and simply go around the form. Continue to add vines, twist around, and tuck in ends, until you are satisfied with its appearance.
3. Finally, try to gently bend each of the original ends up and tuck into the twisting vines. If one should break at this time, just trim it even with the wreath.

Pretzel Heart

Materials needed

clippers
thin to medium-weight long vines
a few vines with natural angles

1. Begin this heart the same way as the giant heart, using an angled vine to make a form. Place the angle on the ground and step on it. Grasp each of the ends of the vine and begin to form the heart curves, but instead of making the center loop, cross and twist the vines over each other into a pretzel shape.

Begin as if you were making a giant heart, but cross and twist the vines in the center instead of making a loop at the point.

Where the vine touches the side, bend it gently to form an angle, and continue wrapping toward the bottom point.

2. Where the vine touches the side, about halfway up from the bottom point, gently give the vine a bend with your fingers to form a slight angle. Tightly twist the rest of the vine around itself going towards the bottom point. You may want to use a piece of masking tape to temporarily keep that angle in place. Do the same with the other side.

3. Using additional vines, twist and wrap them around the heart form as in the other heart constructions. Be sure to twist vines over those side angles to keep them in place. As in the split heart, you may choose to wrap the additional vines over the "pretzel twist" or completely disregard it and just wrap around the outside of the heart form. Continue until the heart is to your liking, then give it a final trim.

🌺 Decorating Suggestions 🌺

Don't go overboard covering up all your hard work with decorations. All you need is a splash of color here and there. Here are some suggestions:

- Attach a simple paper twist bow. It comes in many colors, is easy to work with and is weather resistant.
- Spray paint your wreath to match your decor.
- Peel off all the bark and clip off all the tendrils for a smooth, clean, wooden look. Or leave the short twigs in the tendrils and the shaggy bark as is for a rough, rustic, primitive look.
- To achieve a wild look, keep adding pieces of vine with lots of nice tendrils, and pick out or stretch out any tendrils caught up between the vines.
- Turn a full, thick wreath into a unique table centerpiece. Lay it flat and use it to hold hors d'oeuvres on toothpicks with a bowl of dip or sauce in the center. Or place a fat candle in the center with hurricane glass over it.
- Collect bird nests, feathers, reindeer moss, lichens, shells, nuts, pine cones, berries, twigs, bark, seed pods, reeds, and grasses for free, natural decorations.
- Small toys, wooden decorations, Christmas ornaments, and dolls make unique additions to wreaths.
- Using a grapevine wreath as a base, overwrap it with another vine of a different texture and color such as bittersweet or Virginia creeper.
- Use a round or oval wreath to frame a mirror.
- Cut out old greeting cards, photographs or calendar pictures. Glue onto stiff cardboard and frame with a grapevine wreath.
- Add dried herbs from your garden or dried autumn field and meadow flowers such as Queen Anne's lace, Joe Pye weed, St. John's wort, yarrow, rabbit's foot clover, sweet everlasting, tansy, black-eyed Susan, or bee balm.

MAKE A FALL BITTERSWEET WREATH

To make a fall bittersweet wreath, use a grapevine wreath as the base. Lay the bittersweet in a circle on top of the grapevine like a crown. Using a long single piece of grapevine, lace it in and out over the bittersweet so it is lashed to the wreath. This way the bittersweet isn't being moved around, disturbing the beautiful berries. Also, when the season is over or the berries have faded, the bittersweet can easily be taken off by undoing the thin grapevine. Now decorate the wreath for Christmas by tucking in a few pine branches and some holly or winterberry. Wire on a few pine cones and add a red bow.

Now that you have learned to make a variety of wreaths, put your creative wheels into motion. Wreaths and rings of all shapes and sizes can be joined, stacked, lashed, and intertwined to make baskets, trees, and sculptures of all kinds. Countless designs are possible; there is nothing you can't try!

Just remember to have fun, don't worry about perfection, and you'll enjoy your original masterpiece for years to come.

Related Titles of Interest from Storey Communications, Inc.

At Home with Herbs: Inspiring Ideas for Cooking, Crafts, Decorating and Cosmetics by Jane Newdick
An inspiring yet practical volume packed with over 100 herbal projects. Crafters, home decorators, chefs, and naturalists will enjoy the many projects from scented candles and sachets to garlands and topiaries, to beads and cordials, to bath oils and lotions. Plus information on planting harvesting, and storing herbs. 224 pages ISBN 0-88266-886-2

Herbal Treasures: Inspiring Month-by-Month Projects for Gardening, Cooking and Crafts by Phyllis V. Shaudys
A compendium of the best herb crafts, recipes, and gardening ideas. Gardeners, cooks, and craftspeople alike will find a vast array of projects and recipes to try. The month-by-month approach enables the reader to find creative ideas year-round. Extensive reference materials include gardening and craft suppliers. 320 pages ISBN 0-88266-618-5

How to Make Raffia Hats, Bags & Baskets by Liz Doyle
It's surprisingly easy to use raffia! Liz Doyle introduces the reader to the basics of working with raffia and then provides step-by-step instructions for creating dozens of projects. Dyeing, weaving, and embroidery personalize the projects including: sunhats, children's hats, sou'wester, carry bags, and coiled baskets. 64 pages ISBN 0-88266-887-0

Country Crafts: From Storey's Country Wisdom Collection by Editors of Storey Publishing
Step-by-step directions for making quilts and curtains; braiding and hooking rugs; making baskets and clay pots; stencilling walls and floors; weaving caned, rush, and splint seats. 160 pages ISBN 0-88266-628-2

Natural Baskets, edited by Maryanne Gillooly
Basketry techniques include weaving, twining, coiling, braiding, and stitching of natural materials. Many of the more than 20 projects are suitable for the novice basketmaker. 160 pages ISBN 0-88266-793-9

STOREY COMMUNICATIONS, INC. • 1-800-441-5700
8:30 am to 10:00 pm • 7 Days a Week
For ordering information, please see the back cover.